The
BASICS

GOD.
You.
Jesus.
Faith.

Mike Novotny

Published by Straight Talk Books
P.O. Box 301, Milwaukee, WI 53201
800.661.3311 • timeofgrace.org

Printed in the United States of America
ISBN: 978-1-949488-52-4

Contents

There's Something About Jesus 5

GOD 8

You 14

Jesus 20

Faith 29

Conclusion 35

THERE'S SOMETHING ABOUT JESUS

Napoleon Bonaparte once admitted that there was something about Jesus.

It wasn't Jesus' fame that set him apart, although he was, historically, incredibly famous. Nor was it Jesus' teaching about turning the other cheek or treating others as you would like to be treated, although those quotes have been quoted for the past two thousand years.

What was it that made Jesus so magnetic? Napoleon said, "Alexander, Caesar, Charlemagne, and myself founded empires; but upon what foundation did we rest the creations of our genius? Upon force! But Jesus Christ founded His upon love; and at this hour millions of men would die for him." [1]

Love. In a world where all of us—from the quiet teenage girl to the seemingly confident CEO—ache to be loved, Jesus stands out.

Recently, a young woman started coming to the church where I am a pastor. After her first visit, she texted me, "Thought I'd try church cuz I'm an atheist. Starting to like it." After her second visit, she texted again, admitting that she had been struggling with impulsive behaviors and going back to some self-destructive habits. I immediately replied with a message about Jesus' love and willingness to forgive, telling her that our church was filled with people who had battled/were still battling addictions.

Her response? "Now that I keep going to church, I believe there is a God and Jesus will forgive me of my sins. Hard to wrap my head around sometimes."

My response to her response? "I can't tell you how much I love this text. It's still hard for me to wrap my head around the fact that Jesus forgives me for my sins. I don't deserve it, but he still did it."

Her response to my response to her response? "I almost cried last service because you talked about how he unconditionally loves us enough to have been there for us."

---

[1] William J. Federer, *America's God and Country: Encyclopedia of Quotations* (St. Louis: AmeriSearch, 2001), 463.

My response to her response to my response to her response? "Boom!"

I love moments like that, the times when I see the love of Jesus through fresh eyes as people hear about him for the very first time and are drawn to hear more. That's what kept her coming back, and that's what keeps me reading the Bible, going back to church, and talking to Jesus in my prayers.

How about you?

I'm not sure how this book ended up in your hands. Maybe you were just watching TV or scrolling through social media when something got your attention, causing you to slow your scroll long enough to truly listen. Or maybe you just got done with church and there was something unique about the message, something that surprised you about God or moved you about Jesus, and you picked up this book as a next step. Or maybe your life is a mess right now, and you're sitting in jail or staring at the wine bottle you polished off personally last night, and you know you need a new chapter in your life before it is too late. Or maybe you've realized, like billions of people before you, that there is something missing in your life. You've binged the latest shows, bought the latest stuff, upgraded your life in a dozen ways, but it hasn't been enough to satisfy your soul and give your life a true direction and purpose.

Whatever got these words in front of your eyes, I am grateful you are here. And I imagine you have questions! I know my neighbor does.

There is a guy who lives right next door to our church, close enough that I could kick a soccer ball from my parking spot and hit his bedroom window. He and I just seem to click, so I love talking to him about life, work, and family. In recent months, he has even accepted my invitation to check out our church and listen to our messages about God, Jesus, and faith.

Recently, however, he admitted to me, "I feel like I'm starting in the middle of the movie."

Maybe you have felt that way too. You can be a very intelligent person and yet be very overwhelmed by all the information in an average church service or on any given page of the Bible. While you've likely heard the names Peter, Mary, and Jesus, you might not be so sure about Isaac, Isaiah, and the 17 other Marys who show up in the story. Add to that the church lingo like *grace, faith, saved, holy, glory, worship,* your "walk with God," and all the other insider language that Christians use, and you can feel pretty out of place.

Or maybe, while the pastor talks about the Bible's plan for dating or parenting, you have more basic questions:

- What is God like?
- What does God think of when he thinks of me?
- What exactly was Jesus all about?
- How do I "get saved," and what precisely does "get saved" mean?
- What should I do next?

If you feel sheepish asking such basic questions, please don't be embarrassed. Plenty of other people in history did the exact same thing.

When Jesus' friend Peter spoke to a massive crowd about the Christian faith, they responded, "What shall we do?" (Acts 2:37[2]). And when a military man realized that he had some serious spiritual issues, he asked a Christian named Paul, "What must I do to be saved?" (Acts 16:30).

Questions like that are why I wanted to write this book. One of the best things about the Christian faith is its oceanlike depth. After 40 years of following Jesus, I still discover new things in the depths of the Bible. Yet just like the ocean, there are basic truths that even first-time listeners can enjoy, like a child who giggles as she builds sandcastles at the edge of the water.

This book won't answer every question you have about God, Jesus, or faith. But I hope it helps you dip your toes in the water and experience the refreshing love that has captivated the hearts of billions of people.

So let's spend some time learning who God is, who you are, what Jesus did, and what faith has to do with it. God. You. Jesus. Faith.

Ready to discover the truths that have changed the world?

[2] If you don't know what *Acts 2:37* means, the Bible is broken up into books (like Acts) that have chapters (like chapter 2), which have verses (like verse 37). The shorthand way of saying that is, "Acts 2:37." We do the same thing with cities, streets, and addresses to find the way to a specific destination more easily.

GOD

Last week I had coffee with a gentleman whose body, according to two medical professionals, was "trash."

After a long career in the utilities industry, he had suffered a shoulder injury that left him incapable of lifting 15 pounds much less doing the hard labor that his job required. Further south, his knees had imitated his shoulders, grinding down and wearing old, leaving him attached to a cane that sat on the table as we talked.

The mouth attached to this worn-out body explained to me how demoralizing it was to sit at home and do nothing, to watch another show and listen to another headline, a new normal that had left him depressed and lost.

"But," the man smiled, after his catalog of suffering, "GOD is here!"

This guy knew his audience well, since I had just written a book about those same three words.[3] And he already knew my favorite way to think about the "big Guy upstairs," not as a generic "god" or an official "God" but as a glorious, wonderful, indescribable "GOD!"

GOD is where I want our journey to begin. As much as I am tempted to jump into you and Jesus, I don't think Christianity will make much sense (or seem all that urgent) unless we slow down and think about GOD.

(Don't worry. After a few pages, you won't be annoyed that I keep leaving the caps lock on.)

When you hear that name—GOD—what do you think? What do you envision in your mind? What happens in your heart?

Honestly, those are awkward questions. We can't see GOD, so it's hard to know exactly what to think about GOD. Even the Bible admits that GOD is "the King . . . invisible" (1 Timothy 1:17), which means we can't see him, meet him, and get to know him in the same way we would a guy at work or a girl from our school.

Thankfully, GOD gives us some help in understanding what he's like. And you don't need to be a Bible expert to get it.

---

[3] *3 Words That Will Change Your Life*, just in case you're looking for a book to read after this one.

GOD is even better than _____.

If I could slow down your page-flipping for a second, could I ask you to find a pen and a piece of paper? (You can scribble in this book too.[4])

I would love for you to write down the last five moments in your life that made you really happy. Think of the people who made you laugh, the places that made you gasp, or the things that made your day. Dates, dogs, songs, shows, donuts, days off—anything is fair game. Go ahead.

1._____

_____

2._____

_____

3._____

_____

4._____

_____

5._____

_____

I love doing this exercise too, even as a longtime follower of Jesus. Here's what I wrote down today:

1. I had a blast playing Zelda on the Nintendo last night while my family was asleep.[5]

---

[4] Unless this book belongs to your local library. I would hate to lead you into a life of crime.

[5] No judging, okay? Forty-something men have a special place in their hearts for Zelda.

2. My preteen daughter shared the latest Justin Bieber song with me this morning.[6]

3. Someone sent me a really kind email, thanking me for my work.

4. My wife wrapped her arms around me and gave me one of those hugs that you don't want to end.

5. We ate steak quesadillas last night (the ones with the cinnamon/sugar/lime zest rub).

What in the world do pop stars, long hugs, and quesadillas have to do with GOD? And how does your list of recent joy help you "see" the invisible One?

I'm glad you asked.

The apostle Paul, a first-century Christian, explained it this way: "God's invisible qualities—his eternal power and divine nature—have been clearly seen, being understood from what has been made" (Romans 1:20).

Follow Paul's logic. He admits that GOD is invisible, that you can't see his qualities like you could see your friend's (latest) hair color or approximate height. Yet GOD still can be seen, "clearly seen," in fact. How? "From what has been made."

Look around at the world, and you will see glimpses of GOD. You will see love, friendship, faithfulness, comfort, compassion, surprising generosity, breathtaking beauty, undeserved forgiveness, and so much more.

The thrill of seeing a text from someone you like. The relief of hanging out with people you don't have to impress, where you can untuck your shirt and take off your shoes. The comfort of your Saturday sweatpants and the Insta-worthy glory of a sunset at the beach. Hearing your mom say, "I forgive you" after you mess up. Or your husband comment, "We're going to get through this" when you think your marriage is over. Falling in love. Being loved. Seeing evidence of someone's personal love for you.

All these good moments are great ways to think of the greatest one of all—GOD.

---

[6] What did I say about no judging?

Christians believe the basic logic that GOD is better than
_____. Seeing a video of a clumsy puppy
makes you instantly happy, and GOD is better than a puppy.
Being invited to hang out after work feels really good, and GOD
is better than your coworkers. Gasping at the blazing stars
on a country night is a spiritual experience, and GOD is even
better than the stars. Feeling so close to someone, so loved by
someone, and the love of GOD is better than the love of your best
friend, the greatest mother, or your significant other.

Those moments are GOD's way, through nature, of telling
you what he is like. Obviously, they don't last forever (I can eat
a donut fast!), but they are temporary glimpses of GOD. They
are his ways of shaking any small thoughts out of your head and
making his name—GOD—as big and beautiful as it should be.

This view of GOD was the shared belief of people like
Jesus' friend John, the apostle Paul (the guy all those "St. Paul"
churches are named after), King David (a b.c. poet and warrior),
and the prophet Moses (who first held the Ten Commandments).
Let me prove it:

- "God is love" (1 John 4:8).
- "God . . . is rich in mercy" (Ephesians 2:4).
- "God is faithful" (1 Corinthians 1:9).
- "This only do I seek . . . to gaze on the beauty of the
  Lord"(Psalm 27:4).
- "Your love is better than life" (Psalm 63:3).
- "The Lord, the Lord, the compassionate and gracious
  God, slow to anger, abounding in love and faithfulness,
  maintaining love to thousands, and forgiving wickedness,
  rebellion and sin" (Exodus 34:6,7).

GOD is loving, merciful, faithful, beautiful, better,
compassionate, gracious, and forgiving. And that was only
six quotes out of the big book we call the Bible! No spiritual journey should start without a clear idea of what GOD is like, and the
Bible tells us that GOD is better than your best thoughts about him.

You don't have to wait until a church service or your next
Bible reading to get to know GOD. Just look around. Lean into
the best moments of life. When you do, your heart will be one
step closer to grasping the incredible character of GOD.

So what?

An old professor once told a class of pastors-in-training, "When you stand up in church to talk, I want you to picture me sitting in the back row. And when you envision me there, I want you to hear me asking one question every Sunday—So what?"

That's a good question. Okay, that kind of GOD sounds pretty incredible, but so what? What does that have to do with your day-to-day life?

Here's my best answer—The presence of a loving person is powerful.

When my wife, Kim, and I got married back in 2003, we didn't move into a mansion. Our first "home" was a little apartment in southeastern Wisconsin with one bathroom and a tiny square kitchen and minimal closet space. We had no garage, meaning we had to scratch off the frost and warm up the cars during those long Midwestern winters.

Were we miserable? Nope. Not even close. Because the presence of a loving person is powerful. We had each other, and that was enough to make those years pretty incredible.

I bet you have experienced that too. Maybe algebra wasn't your idea of a good time, but if you had the right people present in class with you, life was good. Maybe you went through the sweat fest of 5K training or basic training, but if you had good friends by your side, life was good. Maybe it was a miserable week of work, but if your two-year-old gave you the longest, warmest hug in recent history, you quickly forgot about the misery.

The presence of a loving person is powerful.

At its very essence, this is what the Bible is about. It's about you and me being in the presence of the most loving person imaginable, namely, GOD. If the most compassionate, powerful, beautiful, and interesting person in the universe was in the room with us, then our lives would be, well, pretty incredible!

This is what GOD wants. He wants to be with you. He wants to walk through life with you. He wants you to have a place in his presence, a seat at his table, a spot in his kingdom. That, both in this life and the next, is the way to be profoundly content.

An ancient king named David said, "Even though I walk through the darkest valley, I will fear no evil, for you are with me" (Psalm 23:4). These words are often quoted at funerals, offering comfort to grieving loved ones. "You are still with me,

GOD," we think, "so I am going to get through this."

About one thousand years later, a Christian in prison wrote, "I have learned the secret of being content in any and every situation, whether well fed or hungry, whether living in plenty or in want" (Philippians 4:12). What was his secret? The presence of the most loving person: "The Lord [a name for God that emphasizes his love] is near" (Philippians 4:5).

You can say the same thing as David and that imprisoned follower of Jesus. You can say, "Even though I might not get the job I want, I will not be afraid. Even though he might break up with me or we might not be able to conceive, I will not be afraid. Even though I might have to live with anxiety or depression, I will not be afraid. Because GOD is love, and GOD is not going to leave!"

It is possible to be unafraid and content, at peace and filled with joy, if GOD is in the room. If a GOD that good is with you, then you have a good life.

Which begs the bigger question—Is GOD with a person like you?

YOU

Even if we have never met, I have a hunch you and I have the same problem. We're not GOOD.

I'd apologize for the quirky caps lock again, but I want you to know I'm not talking about "good." You might very well be a good person, a relatively decent human compared to the drama queens at work and anger kings online. No, you're not perfect. But you do try to learn from your mistakes, grow in your character, and give more than you take.

That's good. But it's not GOOD. And GOOD is what it takes to be with GOD. The Bible's logic is that GOD is so good that he cannot stand things that are bad. He loves people so much that his very nature cannot put up with evil, even a little evil sprinkled in here or there or that one bad thing buried deep in your past. GOD knows how much one cruel word can hurt people or how a little anger can ruin a family, so he refuses to put up with it. He is holy. Pure. Unable to stand it when the people he loves are not perfectly loved.

That is one of the best parts about GOD's character (can you imagine if he was cool when people were cruel to you?), but it is also the scary part about him. Because that means GOD has serious issues with parts of your character. He has serious issues with you. I'm not trying to judge you unfairly here. I feel the same way about my own life.

You might, if I gave you the highlights, call me a good person. I read to my kids almost every night, take my wife on a date almost every week, and give strategically to the poor almost every month. That's good, right?

But if I added the lowlights, you might reconsider your judgment. I often get moody about truly trivial things; am too inflexible and addicted to my schedule; and have an instinctive ability to think about what I want, when I want it, and how I want it done. That might be normal by human standards, but my normal still hurts people. And that's not GOOD.

Passages like these make me question just how close to GOOD I actually am:

- "Do not let any unwholesome talk come out of your mouths, but only what is helpful for building others up according to their needs, that it may benefit those who listen" (Ephesians 4:29).

- "But among you there must not be even a hint of sexual immorality, or of any kind of impurity, or of greed, because these are improper for God's holy people. Nor should there be obscenity, foolish talk or coarse joking, which are out of place, but rather thanksgiving" (Ephesians 5:3,4).
- "Do nothing out of selfish ambition or vain conceit. Rather, in humility value others above yourselves, not looking to your own interests but each of you to the interests of the others" (Philippians 2:3,4).

Helpful words. Not a hint of sexual immorality. Be grateful. Be humble. Prioritize others. I don't have to think back to my toddler or teenage years to remember the last time I didn't do the good things on that list.

I'm guessing you could write your own version of this moral inventory, remembering both the noble moments of the past and the days/words/choices you wish you could undo. In fact, since this is so spiritually important, grab your pen again and finish the following sentences:

- People might consider me a good person because I . . .

- But people might change their minds if they knew that . . .

Was it hard to write those last words? I wonder if you hesitated, thinking through who might pick up this book and read your confession. Perhaps you chose the PG-13 version of your past, editing out the R-rated moments that you are ashamed to put into print.

You and I have the same problem. We do some good and perhaps are mostly good, but we are not entirely good. We are not GOOD to an extent that makes us enough to be in the presence of GOD. There is an obvious difference between good at bar league softball and GOOD enough for major league baseball, a clear line between karaoke good and record label GOOD.

We all know that, in some crowds, you have to be more than good. And that is absolutely true for GOD. By his standards, no one is all that GOOD. No one is worthy to stand and soak in his glory.

- "All have sinned and fall short of the glory of God" (Romans 3:23).
- "Without holiness no one will see the Lord" (Hebrews 12:14).

Is GOD's standard high? The highest. We would expect nothing less from someone who cares so much about love that he claims to be love itself. So how is it even possible to reach that standard? How can people like us become GOOD?

About a year ago, a pastor told me about the answer that many elderly people gave to that question. As he stopped by local nursing homes, he frequently asked, "If you died today, do you think you'd be good enough to be with GOD? Are you confident that you would go to heaven?"

Almost always, their gray-haired heads would nod. So the pastor followed up, "How do you know?"

One confident woman replied, "I went to church all these years and paid my dues."

I mean, no offense to one of my elders, but that is an extremely offensive answer. Can you imagine her saying to all the people she hurt in her life, "I might have yelled at you, taken you for granted, argued with you, ignored you, and tried to manipulate you, but I went to church all those years!"

Um, no. Spending an hour in a church does not a GOOD person make.

While you might shake your head at this woman's beliefs, please note that most of us think something similar. We think we're probably going to a better place because we (fill in something good) and didn't (fill in something really bad). We convince ourselves that our "good" should be good enough. Or we compare our goodness to other people, specifically the really bad people, and tell ourselves that GOD must be happy with us and mad at them.

But that's only possible if GOD is God, if he isn't GOOD but just relatively good.

So what?

Okay, so what? So you and I are not GOOD like we should be. We're human. We fall short. We don't always love the way GOD wants us to. What's the big deal with being human?

The big deal is that we are in serious danger of being separated from GOD.

That is what sin does. *Sin* is the simple word the Bible uses to describe our thoughts, words, and actions (or lack of actions) that don't line up with what the GOD of love wants. Whenever we replace love with sin, it separates people. Like two repelling magnets, sin pushes us apart so that the person who was once right here ends up over there.

You have experienced this, right?

Your dad was overbearing and verbally abusive. Maybe he self-medicated his loneliness with a six-pack of Pabst and took out his unsatisfied soul on you. And what did his sin do? Made you want to run away. Made you hide in your room. Made you long for a reason to get out of the house.

Because sin separates.

Your best friend in high school broke your trust. You thought you could tell her anything, so you did. But one day, desperate for attention from someone she admired, your friend betrayed you. And what did her sin do? Made you want to avoid her locker. Made you find a new place to sit at lunch. Made you look for a new ride home after school.

Because sin separates.

You got into it with someone at church. A meeting of Christian men got rather unchristian. Love got lost in a battle of strong wills. And what did all that sin do? Made you want the meeting to end. Made him avoid the next Sunday handshake. Made you think about finding a new church or give up on going to church altogether.

Because sin separates.

Paul, the guy who gushed about GOD's bottomless love, wrote this to the Christians in Rome: "The wages of sin is death" (Romans 6:23).

What you get for your sin is death. What happens when you don't love is that you don't get to be with the GOD of love. He is too GOOD to be in the presence of that. He is ashamed of sin. He doesn't belong around it.

This was never GOD's original plan. When he created us, he made us morally perfect, which allowed us to live in his presence. People could walk with GOD because they were much like GOD. However, things fell apart at what some Christians call "the fall," the moment when sin entered the world and our resemblance to GOD was shattered like a broken mirror. Like it or not, you and I entered the story post-fall, in a world that is stuffed with the sin that separates us from GOD and from one another.

You might be pushing back on that claim because you don't feel like you deserve to be judged so harshly. But the truth is that you do deserve it. You and I deserve to be held accountable for the bad things we have done, regardless of how many good things we may often do.

Imagine you are sitting in court with the man who killed your best friend in a tragic drunk driving accident. After a few birthday shots, this man got behind the wheel, drifted over the yellow line, and left your best friend's mother to grieve for the rest of her life.

But the defendant's lawyer stands up and tries to reason with the judge: "Your Honor, my client is a good man. He has spent 53 years on this earth and has only driven while intoxicated on one occasion. One single night. That means that since his 16th birthday, he has driven sober 13,504 days and driven drunk just once. By my math, he has been a good driver 99.99 percent of his life. And, Your Honor, my client has never once robbed a bank or abused a child or committed a hate crime. He has kept 99 percent of this nation's laws 100 percent of the time. Therefore, I believe it is obvious he is a good person who does not deserve to be punished in any way."

How would you feel about that defense? I bet you would be furious. Because you're not looking for percentages or averages. You're looking for justice. You care about the one night, the one choice, the one sin that separated your friend from his family.

Get my point? GOD is not concerned about your moral batting average. As a GOD of constant love, he can't stand it when people aren't loved. Even once.

This is the obvious problem that most people would rather not think about, but I hope you do. All of us have a court date coming with GOD, so what will we say to him? How will we defend ourselves? How will we dare to claim that we deserve to go to a better place? How, in this life, will we possibly believe that a pure GOD of love is with us?

I realize these are disturbing questions to think about seriously. You might even be regretting the fact that you picked up this book. But the Christian faith, once the sobering news about sin has set in, offers what no one else in the universe does—an answer. A way for people like us to get back into the presence of GOD, now and forever.

That's what Jesus is all about.

JESUS

If you don't think Jesus is a big deal, just check the date on your calendar.

The year listed is a subtle reference back to Jesus, to the approximate time that he lived, died, and (as we will discuss) came back to life.[7] However, these are far more than interesting historical moments. They are the only way for GOD and you to get back together.

I'm not sure how much you know about Jesus of Nazareth. Perhaps you know he was a first-century religious leader who launched one of the largest movements in world history, what we call Christianity. You might have heard some of his quotes about turning the other cheek (Matthew 5:39) or going the extra mile (Matthew 5:41). If you have some church experience, you might even know his mother's name (Mary), his birthplace (Bethlehem), and the way he died (on a cross).

But who exactly was Jesus? And what was the purpose of his life?

You can read the entire history in Matthew, Mark, Luke, and John (the four biographies about the life of Jesus that are in the Bible), but here's a summary of what Jesus is all about.

Jesus' birth

The first witnesses of the birth of Jesus were blue-collar, third-shift shepherds who probably hadn't showered in weeks. It was an otherwise average night of staring at sheep when a messenger came with breaking news: "Today in the town of David a Savior has been born to you; he is the Messiah, the Lord. This will be a sign to you: You will find a baby wrapped in cloths and lying in a manger" (Luke 2:11,12).

And a baby in a manger was exactly what they found. A few miles south of Jerusalem, in the little town of Bethlehem (aka "the town of David"), a poor woman named Mary pushed out her firstborn, a son. Her fiancé, a carpenter named Joseph, was at her side. The Bible doesn't say exactly what Joseph did or

---

[7] If you could predict and then pull off your own resurrection, we might change the calendar for you too!

said on that night, but I picture him as wide-eyed and helpless as a deer frozen by oncoming headlights.

What mattered most wasn't Joseph or Mary, but the baby lying in a manger. His name? Jesus.

He was, in thousands of respects, like you at your birth. Small; helpless; sevenish pounds of skin, bones, and developing brain. He cried, needed to be changed, and cost Mary more than a few nights of good sleep. Jesus was, as some Christians would later put it, "true man."

But in other ways, Jesus was not at all like you. Remember what the messenger said to the shepherds? "A Savior has been born . . . the Messiah, the Lord."

A Savior is someone who saves, that is, someone who rescues another person from danger. As we would come to find out, Jesus would rescue people like us from the danger of not being GOOD enough for GOD. While he would certainly become famous as a good teacher, a powerful healer, and an influential leader, the first title on his résumé was Savior. GOD in heaven sent Jesus to meet the greatest need of humankind, namely, to be saved from the sins we could not undo—the sins that separate us from God.

The next title was "the Messiah." *Messiah* is a fancy word that comes from Hebrew that essentially means "the One." The word *Christ* means the same thing in the Greek language, which is why some people call Jesus the Messiah and others just call him Jesus Christ.

But what does "the One" imply? Jesus was the One whom GOD had been promising to send ever since humanity stopped being GOOD. The Old Testament (all the books in the Bible that come before the birth of Jesus) made dozens, if not hundreds, of promises about the Messiah, including where he would be from, what he would do, and how he would restore the broken relationship between sinful people and a sinless GOD.

In other words, the baby in the manger was GOD's chosen One, the only One who could save people from their spiritual dilemma.

Finally, Jesus was called "the Lord." What a claim! The baby Jesus, so frail he couldn't yet flip himself over onto his tummy, was also the Lord. He is, somehow, GOD. This is why one of Jesus' nicknames was Immanuel, a Hebrew name that means "God with us."

If your brain hurts right now, that's okay. There is no one else like him whom you can compare him to. You and I have met plenty of humans and, perhaps, we have talked to the invisible GOD of heaven, but we have never seen GOD with us, in a body, in human flesh.

But that's exactly what Jesus was.

One of the earliest recorded songs about Jesus was already being quoted in the mid-first century. Its lyrics said about him, "[Jesus], being in very nature God, did not consider equality with God something to be used to his own advantage; rather, he made himself nothing by taking the very nature of a servant, being made in human likeness" (Philippians 2:6,7).

Jesus was GOD, yet he was made in human likeness. GOD and man in one person. The GOD-man.

It makes you wonder—If the GOD who hates sin and loves love came to this earth, what would he do? What would he do to people like us?

Thankfully, we have answers to those very questions.

Jesus' life

If I had to summarize the life of Jesus in one word, I would choose the word *unexpected*.

You might not expect Jesus to spend the first 30 years of his life in a backwoods village in northern Israel, but that's exactly what he did, spending almost 90 percent of his life in Nazareth. You might not expect him to invest his childhood, teenage years, and 20s working as a carpenter and being a good neighbor, but that's exactly what he did, not beginning his work of teaching about spiritual things until he was around 30 years old. You might not expect him to hang out with questionable characters like prostitutes and divorcées, but that's exactly what he did.

Jesus of Nazareth said unexpected things, went to unexpected places, and surrounded himself with unexpected people.

But as GOD among us, the one expected thing that he did was love people.

If you've ever heard of a church named Saint Matthew's or Saint Peter's or Saint Mary's, that's because Jesus loved sketchy people like Matthew, Peter, and Mary. Matthew was a former tax collector, a scandalous job in first-century Israel that involved working for the enemy and squeezing money out of your own people for personal gain. Peter was a fisherman who had foot-in-mouth syndrome and a tendency to let his anger and emotions get the best of him. Mary Magdalene (one of the many Marys in the Bible) was in a dark spiritual place when Jesus met her, yet he still invited her to follow him. She became one of his closest friends.

Jesus loved the unlovable. Don't think of him as a pushover, however. Jesus was fiercely protective of children and confronted sin boldly, proven by his willingness to call out publicly his own friends, church leaders, and local pastors who weren't being as GOOD as they should.

To be honest, when you read everything the Bible says about his life, it is hard to put Jesus in anyone's corner. He sacrificed constantly to care for the poor, yet his standards for marriage and sexuality were very traditional. In one breath he would tell the crowds they needed to live under the spiritual authority of the church, but in the next breath he would blast the hypocrisy of the leaders of the church. In one message he spoke of loving your enemies and refusing to judge others, but in another message he insisted on the existence of hell and the need for every person to be saved from their own bad behavior.

I struggle to find the words to summarize the life of Jesus because Jesus lived such an unexpected life. A surprising life. A life unlike any other that has ever been lived. But I can say that through all his years on earth, there is one thing that Jesus always was—GOOD. In all his words and his works, Jesus never fell short of that standard. He never sinned. He never did anything to cause his Father in heaven to turn his face away or keep his distance.

Even Jesus' enemies couldn't accuse him credibly. Once, when they dragged him into court and demanded the death sentence, the judge cried out, "Why? What crime has he committed?" (Matthew 27:23).

The answer was none. Because Jesus was GOOD. Because Jesus was GOD.

It turns out that the GOODness of Jesus is really good news for people like us, especially if you understand what happened when he died.

Jesus' death

In the late 1800s in Japan, a man named Sokichi murdered his employer's son during the course of a robbery. He was caught, condemned, and sentenced to death on a cross, where a picture was taken of the execution. Unless you have a weak stomach, I'd encourage you to search for "Sokichi cross" and see, with your own eyes, the kind of death that Jesus died.

While we are used to seeing crosses on churches, in fashion, and on jewelry, in Jesus' day, the cross caused people to shudder. The Romans had perfected the pain of the cross, devising a way to make victims suffer as much as possible and as long as possible. By nailing men to an upright piece of wood, gravity would make every breath an excruciating experience, forcing victims to choose between the pain of suffocation or the pain of pushing themselves up on the nails hammered next to their nerves.

That description should make you shake your head at the thought of the cross' most famous victim of all—Jesus. If Jesus was GOD with us and if Jesus was entirely GOOD, why would he, of all people, die on a cross?

The Bible has two answers, the earthly answer and the spiritual answer.

The earthly answer, which you can read throughout Matthew, Mark, Luke, and John, is that the religious leaders of Jesus' day felt threatened. They hated how Jesus called them out publicly for their bad behavior (aka pride), they despised how many people hung on Jesus' every word (aka jealousy), and they were terrified that the Romans would punish all the Jews in Israel when they dispersed the "mob" that was following Jesus (aka fear). That is why the religious leaders eventually found a way to arrest Jesus secretly, condemn him on false charges, and pressure the Roman governor, Pontius Pilate, to put Jesus on a cross.

Why was Jesus on a cross? The earthly answer is because of them. The insecure priests and leaders of the people. The unjust governor. The betrayer from Jesus' own inner circle.

But the spiritual answer that the Bible gives is not them; it's you. Jesus Christ died on a cross because of you. If it wasn't for you and me, Jesus would not have been on a cross. GOD would not be anywhere close to there. But because of us, that is exactly what happened. The human problem that has existed ever since the fall has put every man, woman, and child in serious spiritual danger because none of us are able to (1) not sin for very long or (2) undo the sins that we have done in the past. That's why Jesus was hanging there. Jesus died for us.

That thought should, in one sense, destroy you. Search for Sokichi's picture again, and then try to picture the GOD of perfect love on a cross. To think that your impatience and my lack of kindness did that is . . . unthinkable. Causing pain to another person is enough to haunt you; imagine causing pain to the only one who is truly GOOD.

But the Bible spends more time talking about the cross as good news, in fact, as the best news in human history. Because there, as Jesus hung on the cross, GOD was saving us. He was dealing with our sins. He was taking care of your every thought and word and action that would prevent you from being GOOD enough to be with GOD.

Slow down your pace and think deeply about each of the following promises related to Jesus' cross:

- "For God was pleased to have all his fullness dwell in [Jesus], and through him to reconcile to himself all things, whether things on earth or things in heaven, by making peace through his blood, shed on the cross" (Colossians 1:19,20).

Must we be separated from GOD? No! Through Jesus, we can be reconciled. The relationship can be fixed. There can be peace through the blood that Jesus shed on that day when he hung on a cross.

- "He forgave us all our sins, having canceled the charge of our legal indebtedness, which stood against us and condemned us; he has taken it away, nailing it to the cross" (Colossians 2:13,14).

What did GOD do with all our sins? He forgave them. How many of them? *All of them*. But what about all the charges GOD could bring against us in his spiritual court? He canceled them. How? By nailing them to the cross.

- "[Jesus] himself bore our sins' in his body on the cross, so that we might die to sins and live for righteousness; 'by his wounds you have been healed'" (1 Peter 2:24).

How do you heal the relationship between you and GOD? "By his wounds." Why doesn't your separating sin get in the way of GOD being close to you? Because Jesus "himself bore our sins." The cross is the cure!

I want to turn this little book into a novel, because the cross means everything! If Jesus had just been a good guy who said some good things about how to follow GOD, you would be stuck with the same problem. In fact, if Jesus had been GOD with us but had only given orders on what to do, what not to do, and how to live, you would be in grave danger. But—thank the Lord!—Jesus is so much more. Jesus is the GOD who came down from heaven to rescue you from danger.

Or, as the shepherds first heard it, "A Savior has been born to you; he is the Messiah, the Lord" (Luke 2:11).

Last week I heard the true story of some followers of Jesus who live in Somalia, a place where believing in Jesus can cost you everything. In one village, secret gatherings are held, where Christians read and remember the glorious truth that GOD is with them because of what Jesus has done for them. When the sun sets, one of the Christians sneaks out of the village and finds a nearby cave, where a Bible is hidden. He retrieves it and sneaks back home, where a small group of excited believers is waiting to read the story again, marveling at a GOD who would give up the safety of heaven and die on a cross for their sins. Once the study is over and before the sun rises, the same man tiptoes back to the cave, hides the Bible, and returns home, knowing that being discovered will mean certain death.

Why does he do it? Because he knows the One who chose death in order to give him life with GOD.

Jesus' resurrection

Imagine if you had a really rich grandma whom you really loved. After a long battle with cancer, Grandma takes her last breath, and, later that year, you find out she has left you a shocking sum of money.

How do you feel?

Well . . . glad . . . and sad. The money will help you, no doubt, but you really miss Grandma.

This is why Jesus is better than your fictional millionaire granny. Not only did Jesus give you an incredible gift at the cross (forgiveness, a chance to be with GOD, etc.). He also showed up soon after his own funeral!

That's right. Jesus rose from the dead.

The Sunday after the Friday that Jesus died, some of his female friends went to grieve at his burial place, an aboveground cave made out of rock. But when they entered, instead of finding their dead friend, they found a living messenger, just like the one who had appeared to the shepherds decades earlier. This messenger told them that Jesus was no longer dead but was alive and breathing, just like he had promised.

Here's what happened next: "So the women hurried away from the tomb, afraid yet filled with joy, and ran to tell his disciples. Suddenly Jesus met them. 'Greetings,' he said. They came to him, clasped his feet and worshiped him" (Matthew 28:8,9).

Why did they worship Jesus? Because Jesus was GOD. And because having GOD with you is really good news.

Easter, for many people, is a good excuse to take a day off work and eat an absurd amount of sugar. I'm all about a good nap and a chunk of dark chocolate, but the meaning of Easter is much more than that. Because of Easter, Jesus is alive, defeating even death itself. Because of Easter, death doesn't get the final word but instead is just a pause between this life and seeing GOD face-to-face.

No wonder Jesus' followers, even today, love Easter Sunday. In fact, every Sunday is a chance for us to gather and remember the glorious things that Jesus did for us through his life and death and resurrection.

You can join us in that joy.

Your life might be filled with ups and downs, moral victories and epic failures, good works and bad choices, but none of that needs to get in the way of you drawing near to GOD. If Jesus lived for you, died for you, and rose from the grave to prove to you that it was true, then there is hope for you!

Here is how Jesus' friends put it:

- "And if Christ has not been raised, your faith is futile;

you are still in your sins. But Christ has indeed been raised from the dead" (1 Corinthians 15:17,20). Without Jesus, you are still "in your sins," a phrase that means you can't escape the sins that separate you from GOD. But since Jesus was raised from the dead, the situation has changed! You are forgiven by the Savior who died and rose for you.

- "[Jesus] was delivered over to death for our sins and was raised to life for our justification" (Romans 4:25). Your sins were handed over to Jesus, and he took them all to the cross. Then, on the following Sunday, Jesus was raised to life for our justification, a fancy word that means GOD doesn't condemn us anymore. We are free to live with him, now and forever.

- "For I am convinced that neither death nor life, neither angels nor demons, neither the present nor the future, nor any powers, neither height nor depth, nor anything else in all creation, will be able to separate us from the love of God that is in Christ Jesus our Lord" (Romans 8:38,39). Nothing in your life, past or future, can stop GOD from loving you.

That's the power of Jesus. He takes away every last one of your sins and presents you as a GOOD person, GOOD enough to make GOD smile when he sees you. And when your last breath comes, there will be nothing to make GOD angry with you, since Jesus has taken care of every offensive thing you have done.

A GOD who likes you. A GOD who is with you. A GOD who listens to you. A GOD who has plans for you. A GOD who will never abandon you. A GOD who will always accept you. A GOD who forgives you. A GOD who will heal you. A GOD who will deliver you from your pain. A GOD who will welcome you with open arms.

None of those sentences could be true without Jesus. But with Jesus, they can be true. In fact, they are absolutely true for everyone who has faith.

So let's dig into the meaning of that essential word—*faith*.

FAITH

Just weeks after his resurrection, with his mission fully accomplished, Jesus returned to heaven. What happened next? Jesus' closest followers, called the apostles, told everyone who would listen about GOD, about how sin separates us from him, and about Jesus. Their hope? That people would believe their message and trust what Jesus did for them was true.

Here's one of the most famous examples about Paul and Silas, two leaders from the early Christian church, who spoke to a prison guard who was suddenly terrified that he was not good enough to be with GOD.

"The jailer called for lights, rushed in and fell trembling before Paul and Silas. He then brought them out and asked, 'Sirs, what must I do to be saved?'" (Acts 16:29,30). What do you think Paul and Silas said? Did they give him a checklist of good things to do? a list of commandments to keep? a minimum requirements for heaven overview?

No (thank GOD!). They gave him Jesus.

"They replied, 'Believe in the Lord Jesus, and you will be saved'" (Acts 16:31). Just believe. Just trust. Just rely on Jesus for everything—for your forgiveness, for your salvation, for your future. It's all about Jesus!

It still is. Doing good things is a vital part of following Jesus, but doing good isn't what you do to get saved. While that might seem logical, it's actually terrifying. The pressure is on you, and you would be doing good things for a bad reason just to avoid missing out on heaven. You would never know if you were good enough.

This is why Jesus did everything for you. Believe that. Trust in him. He will inspire you to do good, not as a way to work your way up to GOD but instead as a way to thank GOD for doing the work to get to you.

There is a fancy word for all this that you may have heard—*repent.*

Repent

The word *repent* might make you nervous. For many people, it is connected to a red-faced, angry, Bible-thumping guy in a suit who probably didn't have many friends in middle school. He's angry. He's yelling. That's repentance.

But that's not entirely true. In fact, it's almost entirely not true.

Back in Jesus' day, the word *repent* simply meant to change your mind about something. You used to think one way, but now you think a different way. That's "repentance." Perhaps you used to think it was okay to _____, but now you believe that behavior is not okay. Or maybe you used to believe that God was like _____, but now you believe that God is like _____.

If you want to be technical about it, repentance has two parts. The first part is about sin, and the second part is about Jesus. Specifically, to repent means to believe that your sin is deadly serious, having the power to separate you from GOD forever, and to believe that Jesus is absolutely incredible, having done everything to get you back to being with GOD forever.

That's what the early Christians said to their neighbors after the death of Jesus. "You all thought putting Jesus on a cross wasn't a big deal, but it was! That was GOD's only Son, and you killed him! Change your mind and agree that you have sinned. You deserve the anger of GOD. But don't despair! Jesus died for you and rose from the dead to prove that it's true. Change your mind and agree that you are forgiven through Jesus."

That's repentance. Change your mind and agree with GOD. If you've read this far, it's very possible that GOD has already changed your mind about those two things!

Human nature wants to edit the first chapters of this book. We tend to consider ourselves better and less sinful than we actually are. As a result, Jesus becomes nice and not necessary, a good teacher who can give us some tips on moral living but not a Savior who rescues us from the danger of missing out on happiness forever.

Which is why Christians are people who repent. They change their minds about all those things and agree that sin is worse than we thought but Jesus is better than we previously believed.

But when you think about it, this is really good news. I might smile when I tell people to repent, urging them to see GOD as more glorious and Jesus as the best gift the world has ever received. There is a way to be saved! There is a way to be safe from shame and sin and hell. His name is Jesus! Repent—change your mind—and you will be good with GOD forever.

Here is how Jesus himself put it—"Repent and believe the good news!" (Mark 1:15).

If that weren't enough, GOD even promises to change us from the inside out, to transform our hearts so that they see his beauty, his love, and his power. This is why repentance is sometimes described as a gift.

What a gift!

I think of the young man who used to wait in the church lobby while his family worshiped inside. Honestly, I didn't expect any spiritual breakthroughs with a teenager who watched YouTube videos with his earbuds in and wasn't interested in even giving Jesus a chance.

But one day he took the earbuds out.

The message he heard intrigued him, so he decided to join his family in church. I can still see him sitting in the front row, barely blinking, leaning in like he didn't want to miss a single word. Then the questions came, questions about creation, salvation, different religions, everything. Our other pastors and I answered them the best we knew how and prayed that God would change his heart so he would agree with Jesus.

And he did!

I remember the day we played a video of his story, hearing how a kid who initially thought Jesus was just a story now saw him as his Savior. Everything had changed. Especially his heart.

That is the beautiful gift of repentance.

So what (now)?

Perhaps your heart is nodding as you read this chapter. "I think I did repent. Something is different. I'm not thinking exactly like I did before about GOD, about myself, and about Jesus. But what now?"

I'm glad you asked.

The honest answer is that you now get to spend the rest of your life going deeper into the things you've read about in this book. Day by day, you'll experience beauty and satisfaction and pleasure and think, "GOD is even better than this!" Moment after moment, you'll struggle with denying yourself, doing what you want, and instead trust in the life that GOD has planned for you, a life filled with loving others as GOD first loved you. Night after night, you'll come back to Jesus, thankful that he took away every sin so you'd never have to fall asleep ashamed.

Like a child growing to maturity, that will take time. Like a tree that starts as a seed and turns into a mighty oak, it won't happen by next Tuesday. But over time, GOD will change you until that day when everything changes and you pass from this life to the next, when you will see his face and say, with more joy than ever before, "GOD!"

Until that day comes, what should you do? I would suggest two key things—GOD's Word and GOD's people.

GOD's Word

The best way GOD changes our minds and gives us faith is through the Bible. The apostle Paul, an early Christian who radically changed his mind about Jesus, once wrote, "Faith comes from hearing the message" (Romans 10:17).

Recently, my family and I got reservations for Easter brunch at a local restaurant where a buffet of sausage links, eggs, and fried chicken awaited us after church. As we stood in line in front of the sausage (my favorite station), the server squinted and asked, "Do I know you from somewhere?"

"Maybe *Time of Grace*, the TV show?" I suggested.

"Yes!" he beamed. "My wife and I have been watching every week." But then he grew suddenly reflective. "Thank you, Pastor. You've helped us. You don't know, but . . ."

I never got to hear the end of that sentence since the buffet line was stacking up behind me, but this 15-second conversation reminded me how lives change when people hear GOD speaking through his Word regularly.

So your number-one goal should be to get as much of the message as you can. In the Bible, GOD has chosen to speak to us, to let us know what he thinks about us and how he uses all things in life, even the hard things, to work out his unique plan for our lives.

I'm not suggesting you quit school, give up your career, and live in the woods with a Bible. I am, however, encouraging you to start some habits that keep you connected to GOD so you can hear his voice, remember his promises, and stay charged up in your faith.

For the past 25 years, I have tried to do that by reading the Bible every day.

Every day I spend some time in the Bible, reading and rereading small sections, underlining stuff that jumps out at me, and asking questions about things I don't understand. I'm not lying when I say that after a quarter century of reading the same book, I am not bored. GOD always has something brilliant to say to me, something that applies so perfectly to my day, which is why I love his Word so much.

So get yourself a Bible or download a Bible app. I prefer a paper version, since my brain is easily distracted when I have a device in my hands, but you can choose whatever works best for you.[8]

Since you're new, it's going to be a touch overwhelming at first. You won't really grasp all the people, places, and things the first time you read. That's okay. Just stick with it, take notes, and write down questions. You'll be amazed at how much can happen in a few months when you commit yourself to this habit.

Another option would be to find a good daily devotional. A "devotional" is something you read or watch that is based off GOD's Word. Time of Grace loves sharing devotionals, so consider checking out their website or signing up for their daily devotional emails.

Warning! GOD will challenge you, forcing you to reconsider so much of what you previously thought and believed. That's okay! Repentance isn't a bad thing. Agreeing with GOD never is.

GOD's people

Doing life with people who believe the same things about GOD, you, and Jesus is extremely important. Even Jesus had friends who prayed for him in his times of greatest need. You'll need other people too.

Please don't be embarrassed. The reason GOD put other Christians in your life is to help you grow. Christianity is not a competition but a community. You don't have to impress anyone with how much you understand or how well things are going.

[8] Since the Bible was not written in English originally, you'll have to choose which version to read, which can be confusing if you're new. I use the New International Version (NIV), which is what I've quoted in this book.

Just the opposite! In GOD's family, we have the blessing of being real with one another, encouraging one another, and asking honest questions of one another.

This, essentially, is what church is all about. At church, I have the chance to listen to GOD, talk to GOD, and sing praises to GOD alongside the people of GOD. Yes, church people are as messy, flawed, and complicated as you are, but there's something powerful about gathering with them that you simply don't get when you stay at home and try to connect with GOD on your own.

So start looking for a church. Find one that loves the Bible, opens the Bible, and helps you understand the Bible. Don't get distracted by the look of the church or the style of music. Instead, find one that is faithful to the things you have learned so far, one that talks about Jesus a lot, one that doesn't flatter you too much, one that makes GOD as big of a deal as he actually is.

New habits are hard, but make it your goal to go to church every Sunday. Because "faith comes from hearing the message" (Romans 10:17).

As you do this, be hungry for answers and humble enough to ask questions. Bring your list of Bible questions to church and ask someone if you could buy them coffee and search for some answers together. Email the pastor and tell him you're new but would love to learn more about GOD's Word. In my experience, Christian veterans love to help.

With your new "brothers and sisters" in the Christian family, you can learn, grow, and be blessed.

In the end, reading the Bible and connecting with people have the same goal—to get you as close to GOD's heart as possible, giving you faith to believe that the GOD who saved you will also be with you every day of your life.

CONCLUSION

GOD. You. Jesus. Faith.

Let's do a quick review:

GOD—The true GOD is better than the best things in life. He is also the only person who will never leave you, get too busy for you, or grow old and die before you. GOD is constantly with his people, a source of incredible peace and wonderful hope. You can get through anything, even death itself, if you are with GOD.

You—Despite all our strengths, we humans share a fatal flaw, namely, that we are not GOOD like GOD is. Our sins might seem normal by our standards, but they are offensive to the GOD who is entirely GOOD, and they separate us from him. Our hardest efforts and biggest changes cannot change the fact that we all have fallen short. We need someone to save us from that danger, or we stand no chance of being with GOD.

Jesus—Jesus came down from heaven to save us from that separation. Because GOD loved you and longed to save you, he sent his only Son, Jesus, the one who lived a perfect life of love, died on a cross to take away your sins, and rose from the dead to prove that it is true. While his words are inspiring, his works are even more essential. Because of Jesus, your past sins, present struggles, and future death do not have to get the last word.

Faith—Faith is trusting in Jesus. We trust that our sins are serious enough to separate us from GOD, and we trust that those same sins are gone because of Jesus' cross. We trust that Jesus rose from the dead, and we trust that our deaths will not separate us from GOD's love.

When this book began, we asked the question, "How do I get saved?" The simple answer is this—Repent and believe in Jesus. If you do, even if there are a thousand behaviors you still need to change, you are saved. You are safe. You are a child of GOD with an eternity of happiness waiting for you!

We also asked, "What do I do next?" Since faith in Jesus is strengthened by spending time hearing/reading the Bible alongside GOD's people, finding a good church is essential for your faith. And in addition to finding a good church, I hope you continue to use Time of Grace content to help you with your personal study of GOD's Word. While it takes time, just like a tiny seed growing into a towering tree, GOD has promised that he will use his Word and his people to help you become more like Jesus, living a life of love for GOD and for others.

Since the Bible is a big book, there is a lot more to say, but I hope these four ideas have given you a good place to start. Even more important, I hope they have made you more interested than ever in Jesus.

Napoleon was right. There is something unique about Jesus, and that something is love.

So if you are searching for love, love that doesn't come and go, love that doesn't fail, love that is bigger than your biggest sins, love that can save you from death, love that can get you to heaven, love that will defeat every foe, then fix your eyes on Jesus.

Through faith in Jesus, you can and will be with GOD forever.

ABOUT THE WRITER

Pastor Mike Novotny has served God's people in full-time ministry since 2007 in Madison and, most recently, at The CORE in Appleton, Wisconsin. He also serves as the lead speaker for Time of Grace, where he shares the good news about Jesus through television, print, and online platforms. Mike loves seeing people grasp the depth of God's amazing grace and unstoppable mercy. His wife continues to love him (despite plenty of reasons not to), and his two daughters open his eyes to the love of God for every Christian. When not talking about Jesus or dating his wife/girls, Mike loves playing soccer, running, and reading.

ABOUT TIME OF GRACE

Time of Grace is an independent, donor-funded ministry that connects people to God's grace—his love, glory, and power— so they realize the temporary things of life don't satisfy. What brings satisfaction is knowing that because Jesus lived, died, and rose for all of us, we have access to the eternal God—right now and forever.

To discover more, please visit timeofgrace.org or call 800.661.3311.

HELP SHARE GOD'S MESSAGE OF GRACE!

Every gift you give helps Time of Grace reach people around the world with the good news of Jesus. Your generosity and prayer support take the gospel of grace to others through our ministry outreach and help them experience a satisfied life as they see God all around them.

Give today at timeofgrace.org or by calling 800.661.3311.

Thank you!